HIGH NOON READING FLUENCY
LEVEL A

Betty Lou Kratoville

High Noon Books • Novato, California

Available from High Noon Books

High Noon Reading Fluency Program

    Level A   ISBN 1-57128-315-3
    Level B   ISBN 1-57128-316-1
    Level C   ISBN 1-57128-317-X
    Level D   ISBN 1-57128-318-8

Cover design by Jill Zwicky
Interior design by Bonni Gatter

Copyright © 2004, by High Noon Books. All rights reserved. Printed in the United States of America. No part of this publication may be reproduced, stored in a retrieval system, or transmitted, in any form or by any means, electronic, mechanical photocopying, recording or otherwise, without the prior written permission of the publisher, unless otherwise indicated.

2 10 9 8 7 6 5 4 3
0 9 8 7 6 5 4 3 2 1

HIGH NOON BOOKS
A Division of Academic Therapy Publications
20 Commercial Boulevard
Novato, California 94949-6191
800 422-7249
www.HighNoonBooks.com

International Standard Book Number 1-57128-315-3
Order No. 8315-3

TABLE OF CONTENTS

Introduction 4
Program Features 4
Using *High Noon Reading Fluency* 4
Timed Reading Options 6
Using the *Writer's Corner* 7
Exercise 1   Rain 9
Exercise 2   The Sale 10
Exercise 3   Roads 11
Exercise 4   The Doghouse 12
Exercise 5   Rice 13
Exercise 6   The Fireplace 14
Exercise 7   Goats 15
Exercise 8   The Trunk 16
Exercise 9   Plants 17
Exercise 10   Jeans 18
Exercise 11   Coal 19
Exercise 12   Nell Green 20
Exercise 13   Black Bears 21
Exercise 14   Bats 22
Exercise 15   Gold 23
Exercise 16   The Beach 24
Exercise 17   Salt 25
Exercise 18   Seals 26
Exercise 19   Skunks 27
Exercise 20   Splash! 28
Exercise 21   Sharks 29
Exercise 22   Oil 30
Exercise 23   Grapes 31
Exercise 24   The Ditch 32
Exercise 25   Frogs and Toads 33
Exercise 26   The Mole 34
Exercise 27   Ants 35
Exercise 28   The Card 36
Exercise 29   Moss 37
Exercise 30   Snakes 38
Answer Key 39
Answer Sheet 41
Words Per Minute Log 41
Words Per Minute Chart 42

INTRODUCTION

High Noon Reading Fluency is a four level program designed to give students the extra practice they need to help build fluency in reading. Reading fluency is commonly defined as the seamless mastery of speed and accuracy, with the final goal of achieving comprehension. Fluency is a crucial benchmark that defines success in reading, and the instructional key to achieving fluency is to provide students with an abundance of reading opportunities.

Each level of *High Noon Reading Fluency* includes 30 fiction and nonfiction high interest/low reading level passages. Passages are between 200 and 250 words in length and each is followed by five comprehension questions and an optional writing prompt. Students can use the program independently to build their rate and accuracy. Once they reach their target reading rate and demonstrate comprehension, they move to the next level of the program. When used with groups, the program provides opportunities for other activities that build reading fluency: modeling, choral reading, and oral timed reading. These features combine to make *High Noon Reading Fluency* a flexible tool for fluency instruction.

Program Features

Level A of *High Noon Reading Fluency* contains 30 reading exercises designed to help build reading fluency. Each exercise includes the following features:
- Grade 1 reading level
- Reading passage for practice and timed reading
- High-interest nonfiction and fiction topics
- Comprehension questions
- *Writer's Corner* writing prompt for independent writing

Using *High Noon Reading Fluency*

Students Working Independently

High Noon Fluency can be used as a self-directed program in which students move at their own pace. As students become familiar with the format of the book, exercises may be completed independently.

1. Choose the *High Noon Reading Fluency* level most appropriate to each student's ability. The reading levels in *High Noon Reading Fluency* are as follows:

Level A	First grade
Level B	Second grade
Level C	Third grade
Level D	Fourth grade

2. Provide students with a copy of the Answer Sheet found on page 41 of this book. Also provide students with a copy of the Words Per Minute Log found on page 41, which they can use to track their reading rate for each passage.

3. In each exercise, students should silently read through the passage, using a stopwatch or a classroom clock with a second hand. Students can enter their time in the space allowed on their Answer Sheet.

4. Students should then answer the comprehension questions and enter answers on their copy of the Answer Sheet. They can check their answers against the Answer Key, located on page 39 of this book.

5. Students can extend their reading with a short writing exercise based on the *Writer's Corner* writing prompt. Indicate to the students whether or not they should complete this part of the exercise.

6. After completing the exercise, students can refer to the chart on pages 42-43. This chart gives the Words Per Minute reading rate for each passage. They can chart their progress in the Words Per Minute Log.

Periodically review students' Words Per Minute Log. If students are consistently reading passages at the rate expected for their grade level (see table below), or a rate that you select as appropriate for the student, and answering all comprehension questions correctly, move them up to the next level of *High Noon Reading Fluency*.

Expected Reading Rates by Grade Level

Grade	Words Per Minute
1	50-80
2	90
3	100
4	110
5	120
6	125
7 +	130

From the Phonics-Based Reading Test, by Rick Brownell, copyright © 2002: Academic Therapy Publications, Novato CA.

Working with a Group

When working with groups of students, you may want to provide further instructional support with modeled fluent reading, choral reading, and feedback. These supports can enhance your students' efforts and may contribute significantly to their success.

1. **Silent Reading.** Have students read through the entire passage silently, in order to generally familiarize themselves with the content prior to completing their individual silent timed reading.

2. **Model Reading.** You can provide a model of fluent reading by reading aloud the first few sentences of the passage. Read with a steady pace and appropriate expression.

3. **Choral Reading.** Ask students to begin reading the passage aloud. If you are working with a small group, have students take turns reading several sentences each. You may want to read along at intervals in order to reinforce an adequate reading rate.

4. **Repeated Reading.** Once students have finished reading, you may want to have them repeat a reading of several sentences or a paragraph of the passage to further develop fluency.

5. **Comprehension Questions.** Have students use the copied Answer Sheet to complete the comprehension questions that follow the passage. Answers can be checked with the Answer Key on page 39. Take the opportunity to review items missed at this point and return to the passage for further instruction if necessary.

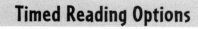

Timed Reading Options

Timed oral reading

You may want to periodically conduct a timed oral reading of a passage. If you are working with a group, time each student apart from the other students.

1. It is recommended that oral timed readings be conducted individually with students and not in a group setting. Use a stopwatch or a classroom clock with a second hand.

2. Tell the student that this is a timed reading and that he or she will be reading the passage out loud. Remind the student to read smoothly and with expression. You may want to model reading rate and expression in the first few sentences of the passage.

3. Have the student find the first word in the passage and place his or her finger on it. Begin the reading by saying **Start** as you start the stopwatch.

4. When the student has difficulty with a word, says he or she does not know the word, or hesitates for up to five seconds, give the word so that the reading is minimally interrupted.

5. Keep a tally of errors. You may want to note words that the student was unable to decode.

Error Type	Student Reads	Examiner Marks
Mispronunciation	Pat has a <u>whit</u> dog.	Pat has a wh*i*te dog.
Insertion	Pat has a <u>big</u> white dog.	Pat has a/white dog.
Omission	Pat has / white dog.	Pat has a̸ white dog.
Substitution	Pat <u>had</u> a white dog.	Pat ha̸s a white dog.
Doesn't Know	Pat has a (<u>don't know</u>) dog.	Pat has a white dog.
Hesitates	Pat has a (<u>hesitates</u>) dog.	Pat has a white dog.

Self corrections should be counted as correct when they are correct. If a correct response is followed by an incorrect self-correction, count the self-correction as an error.

Repetitions should not be scored as errors.

6. When the student has stopped reading, note the time and record the number of errors and number of words. To determine the reading rate for any passage, refer to the Words Per Minute Chart on pages 42-43.

Once the timing is completed, have students continue the exercise, answering the comprehension questions.

Using the *Writer's Corner*

The *Writer's Corner* portion of each exercise is an optional activity that gives students opportunities for independent writing in response to the passage topic. The brief prompts suggest writing activities that enable students to utilize a broad range of writing types to express ideas, opinions, and observations. Students should read the *Writer's Corner* writing prompt provided for each passage. On a separate sheet of paper, they can write their responses to the prompt.

Writing types and some applications

The following are writing types and applications suggested in the *Writer's Corner* writing prompts.

<u>Narrative</u>: Narrative text tells a story, either fictional or nonfiction. Examples of narrative text include:

fictional stories
stories based on historical events
poetry
plays

<u>Responsive</u>: Responsive text contains thoughts, opinions, answers, and feelings that are in response to something read or heard. Examples of responsive text include:

letters to editor
personal essay
personal opinion column
first-person reports

Descriptive: Descriptive text tells about a place, person, process, or idea by providing descriptive details. Examples of descriptive text include:
- journal entries
- letters
- travel articles
- factual reports
- biographies
- directions/instructions

Persuasive: Persuasive text attempts to provide convincing evidence that will persuade the reader to accept the writer's point of view. Examples of descriptive text include:
- letters to editor
- personal essay
- personal opinion column
- advertising copy
- press releases

Exercise 1

Rain

Right now, rain is falling somewhere in the world. About 1,800 thunderstorms take place every hour of the day.

We could not live without rain. All plants must have it. Wild life and livestock must have it. Birds must have it. It means life for all things on Earth.

How do we get rain? It is not hard to understand. The sun warms the air. The warm, moist air rises. This moist air grows colder at it rises. It forms a cloud. Drops form within the cloud. These drops go up with the rising air. They become heavy and fall. These are the first large raindrops that splash on the ground.

The rest of the rain then falls from the cloud.

Sometimes we can have too much rain all at once. Then there is a flood. Homes are swept away. Trees get uprooted. Crops are lost.

Raindrops are not all the same size. The large drops fall faster. Small drops fall much slower. Raindrops wash dust and soot from the air. The world looks clean and fresh again.

We can look in the sky for an arch of red, blue, and pink. Then the sun shines again.

---

1. What needs rain?
   A. Plants
   B. Planes
   C. Buildings

2. A cloud is formed from—
   A. Dust
   B. Moist air
   C. Floods

3. Somewhere in the world it is—
   A. Raining
   B. Snowing
   C. Hailing

4. Raindrops form—
   A. In a cloud
   B. On the ground
   C. When the sun shines

5. We see an arch in the sky—
   A. Last thing at night
   B. After a rain
   C. First thing in the morning

Writer's Corner

Have you been caught in a rain storm? Write what the storm was like.

Exercise 2

The Sale

Joan read that one of the downtown stores was having a big sale. The price on many things had been cut.

"I should go to that sale," Joan said. "I need a swimsuit and a robe." She read the newspaper all the way through. Then she had breakfast. By the time she got downtown, it was almost noon. Joan drove round and round the block. She could not find a place to park her car.

She was getting mad. "I am *not* going to miss that sale," she said. Then she spotted a parking space. Or was it? The curb was red. A sidewalk sign said, "No Parking."

Joan made up her mind. She swung into the open space. "I'll only be a short time. I'll risk it," she thought.

She found a swimsuit. That took part of an hour. She bought a robe. Now she had been in the store for half an hour. She felt good. "I saved a lot of cash," she thought.

She rushed to her car. Uh-oh! What was this? A man was standing there. He looked cross. He was tapping his foot. He held a white slip in his hand.

Joan stuck out her hand. The man gave her the slip. She looked at the slip. "Oh dear," she said. "I guess I didn't save a lot of cash after all!"

---

1. Joan read that the store was—
   A. Closing
   B. Having a sale
   C. Closing late

2. Joan needed—
   A. A pair of new shoes
   B. A swimsuit and robe
   C. Some sweats and socks

3. Joan saw a sign that said—
   A. No Parking
   B. Drive Slowly
   C. No Left Turn

4. Joan parked next to a—
   A. Green curb
   B. Red curb
   C. Yellow curb

5. Joan was in the store—
   A. An hour and a half
   B. Two hours
   C. Half an hour

Writer's Corner

At yard sales used things are sold at a good price. Plan what you could sell at a yard sale.

Exercise 3

Roads

Roads are strips of land for cars, trucks, and bikes to drive on. Most roads are paved and smooth. But there are also dirt roads with deep ruts and bumps.

In towns, roads are called "streets." A town takes care of its own streets. It fixes them when they start to wear out. It keeps them free from snow and ice. Town trucks spread salt or sand on the ice so cars don't skid. Other trucks have blade plows on their front. They push the snow to one side. Drivers are glad when the snow plow gets there before them.

Roads that take lots of cars each day are called highways. They got this name a long time ago. Men tossed dirt from a ditch to build a new road. The road got higher and higher. Soon it was higher than the land on each side. It was called a highway. This word has lasted a long time.

The first roads were trails and paths made by wild life. In fact, roads were not needed until someone made the first wheel. Think of it! Someone shaped a round piece of wood. But how to use it? How about a box on top of two round pieces of wood? What a help that must have been! It was then that trails turned into roads for carts with wheels. And the world changed.

---

1. Most roads are—
   A. Full of holes
   B. Paved and smooth
   C. Unpaved and bumpy

2. When a road is icy—
   A. Drivers stay home
   B. Some walk to work
   C. Trucks spread sand

3. Highways got their name from—
   A. Dirt piled high
   B. Signs placed high over the road
   C. Ditches by the side of the road

4. For many years the only roads were—
   A. Wildlife trails and paths
   B. Highways
   C. Streets in towns

5. Roads were not needed until some one—
   A. Made the first wheel
   B. Built the first mall
   C. Built the first bridge

Writer's Corner

What is the main road you take to get to school? Write the route you take.

Exercise 4

The Doghouse

Nell and Bess sat on the steps of Nell's back porch. Nell's dog Sam lay at their feet.

"There's not much to do today," Nell said.

"You're right. I can't think of a thing," said Bess.

They didn't talk for a while. Then Nell said, "I know what we can do. Let's build a house for Sam."

"How?" asked Bess. "We would need lots of wood and stuff."

Nell stood up. "Our barn is full of things. My dad keeps his tools there."

Nell was right. They found wood in all sizes and tools and nails.

It did not take long to lug the wood and tools outside. They set to work.

"What do you think you're doing?" came a loud voice from the fence.

"It's that pest Dave from next door," Nell said. "Act as if you didn't hear him."

"Girls don't know how to build a doghouse," said Dave.

Nell and Bess didn't say a word. They just kept on pounding nails. At last the job was done.

"Look at your nice new house, Sam," called Nell.

Sam took one look. Then he ran the other way and hid under the back porch.

"Oh, well," Bess said. "I guess we can keep our bats and balls and mitts in it."

---

1. Nell and Bess were sitting—
   A. On a bench in the park
   B. On the steps of Nell's back porch
   C. On the bed in Nell's room

2. Nell and Bess wanted to—
   A. Build a house for Sam
   B. Bake a cake
   C. Go for a walk

3. A loud voice came from—
   A. The barn
   B. The fence
   C. Up the street

4. What happened last?
   A. Sam hid under the porch.
   B. Bess went home.
   C. Dave climbed the fence.

5. What would be the best title?
   A. Building a Doghouse
   B. A Summer Day
   C. The Boy Next Door

Writer's Corner

Do you have a pet? Write a note that tells how to feed and care for your pet for one week.

Exercise 5

Rice

Many in this world eat rice three times a day. They do not have much else to eat. Without rice some would starve.

Almost all rice must be grown in ponds. One kind of rice is called "hill rice." This rice can be grown on hills that get lots of rainfall. Rice likes thick, rich mud to grow in. It is a grass that grows from three to five feet high. At first the rice stands up straight. To get ripe, rice needs warm air between 60° and 80°. When the grain is ripe, the stems bend down. From far away, a rice field looks like a bright green lake.

A rice field is large. Then the farmer cuts the field into small patches. The patches are made with dirt walls. The smaller patches are easy to flood or to drain. The seed is planted with a drill. Sometimes the seed is dropped from a plane!

Rice has many uses. It is fed to livestock. It is put on other plants to make them grow better. Hats, mats, bags, and rope are made of rice straw. Parts of the rice plant are used in drugs to help cure illness.

Rice is a crop grown in almost every part of the world. Where would we be without it?

---

1. Rice must be grown in—
   A. Lakes
   B. Ponds
   C. Fields

2. To get ripe rice needs—
   A. Cold days
   B. Lots of wind
   C. Warm air

3. Rice can be fed to—
   A. Livestock
   B. Bears
   C. Cats

4. Rice is grown—
   A. On a dry island
   B. In all parts of the world
   C. Deep in the forest

5. Many things are made from—
   A. Rice roots
   B. Rice seeds
   C. Rice straw

Writer's Corner

How do you like to eat rice? Write what dish goes best with rice, and how to make it.

High Noon Reading Fluency, Level A

Exercise 6

The Fireplace

It was a cold night. Snow was falling. Wind was blowing.

"How about a fire?" asked Kate's dad.

"Great! I'd love a fire," said Kate. She turned to her twin. "How about you, Ted?"

Ted put down his book. "Sounds fine. What do we do first?"

"We get some newspaper," said Mr. Niles. "Then we bring in some thin sticks of wood from the box in the back hall."

"I'll do that," said Kate.

"Ted, why don't you get some logs from the woodshed?" asked Mr. Niles.

Ted said, "I'm on my way."

Kate and Ted were back in a flash. They watched their dad build the fire. First, the newspapers and next the sticks of wood. Last, Mr. Niles placed three logs on top. "Now all I need is a match," he said.

Mrs. Niles came into the room. "I have a match," she said.

Soon a bright blaze burned in the fireplace. They all sat back and watched the red flames dance. The fire burned down to a soft glow.

Mr. Niles said, "There is something else we need."

"What's that?" Ted asked.

His dad smiled. "Well, it's white and soft and sweet. And you toast it on the end of a stick."

"I know what it is!" Kate ran out of the room.

What do you think Kate will bring back?

---

1. When does this story take place?
    A. In the summer
    B. In the winter
    C. In the spring

2. Who brought the sticks from the back hall?
    A. Kate
    B. Ted
    C. Dad

3. Who brought the logs from the wood shed?
    A. Kate
    B. Ted
    C. Dad

4. Who brought a match?
    A. Dad
    B. Mother
    C. Kate

5. Why did Kate run out of the room?
    A. To go to bed
    B. To get more wood
    C. To find some treats

Writer's Corner

Have you sat outdoors at a campfire to stay warm or tell tales? Write about that time.

Goats

Goats have sometimes been called the "poor man's cow." Like the cow, the goat's milk, meat, hair, and hide are useful. There are both wild and tame goats. Wild goats tend to live in high, rocky places. They can be seen jumping from crag to crag. They do not do well in wet lands.

A grown male goat is called a *buck*. His mate is called a *doe*. If their child is less than a year old, it is called a *kid*. A goat's hair can be short or long. It is white or black or brown or mixed.

We have long heard that goats eat tin cans. That is just a joke. They do not eat tin cans. They do eat a lot of strange things. But most of all they eat grass.

They can find food even on poor dry land. Goats weigh about 120 pounds when they are full grown. They have horns that point backward. Most of them have beards. A goat's milk is white and sweet and rich. It is used often when cow's milk makes a child ill. Fine cheese is made from goat milk.

Goats can be trained as pets. They seem to like pulling a child in a cart.

Goats are like sheep in many ways. We get wool from sheep, We also get wool from goats. Goats need about the same amount of care as sheep. But a sheep is much more fussy about eating than a tough goat.

---

1. A grown male goat is called a—
   A. Buck
   B. Doe
   C. Kid

2. A baby goat is called a—
   A. Buck
   B. Doe
   C. Kid

3. Goats eat a lot of—
   A. Cheese
   B. Tin cans
   C. Grass

4. Wild goats live in—
   A. Swamps
   B. High, rocky places
   C. Thick woods

5. The horns of a goat point—
   A. Backward
   B. Frontward
   C. Straight up

Writer's Corner

Goats are called the "poor man's cow." Write about why goats might have that name.

Exercise 8

The Trunk

Luke hid things. He didn't want anyone, even his mom and dad, to know where he kept his books and toys. He didn't know why. He just liked to keep his own things neat and safe.

One day he found an old wood trunk on the third floor. He bought a lock for the trunk. He was sure all of his stuff would be safe there.

The next day he cut the lawn of the house next door. It was a big lawn. Luke was hot and worn out. The man next door gave him a stack of bills. Luke looked at the cash in his hand. "I must hide this," he thought.

He went to his room. It didn't take long to find an old sock. He stuffed the cash into the sock. He got out the bag where he kept his baseball cards. He put the sock in the bag with the cards. Then he locked the bag in the trunk.

A few days later Luke needed some cash to go to a ballgame. He pulled up the lid of the trunk. What was this? His cash and his cards were in shreds! There was a hole in the trunk. A mouse had got in and chewed a hole in both the bag and the sock. Then he had a feast.

"No more hiding things," said Luke.

---

1. On the third floor Luke found—
   A. Some baseball cards
   B. An old trunk
   C. A lock

2. Luke earned some cash by—
   A. Taking out trash
   B. Cutting a lawn
   C. Sawing wood

3. Luke kept his baseball cards in a—
   A. Bag
   B. Box
   C. Shirt

4. Luke needed cash to—
   A. Buy some books
   B. Help out a pal
   C. Go to a ballgame

5. Luke's cash was spoiled by a—
   A. Fire
   B. Mouse
   C. Flood

Writer's Corner

Make up a tale about a trunk lost from a ship at sea. What was in it? How was it lost?

Plants

Plants are all around us. Most of the time we don't even think about them. Yet we could not live without them. We get most of our food from plants. The meat we eat comes from livestock. That livestock eats plants. We also drink milk. Milk comes from a cow or a goat that eats plants.

We build our homes of wood. Wood comes from a large plant. Look at what you are wearing. Some of it came from a plant.

Long ago, we ate any plant we could find. Later we saw that some plants were better than others. We saved the seeds from these plants. We found soil that was good for the seeds. Soon there were farms.

At least 250,000 kinds of plants grow in the world. All of these fall into four groups. The first group is molds. We see these growing on bread and cheese. Group two is made up of mosses. These have stems but no roots.

Fern plants make up group three. In group four are the plants we know best–trees, grass, shrubs, and the many plants we eat.

Plants grow in strange places. Some are found in hot springs. Some live on snow and ice. Some grow in the dark. Others are at their best in sunlight.

---

1. Plants fall into—
   A. Four groups
   B. Five groups
   C. Three groups

2. One plant group is made up of—
   A. Bread
   B. Cheese
   C. Molds

3. Plant group two is made up of—
   A. Mosses
   B. Stems
   C. Roots

4. Plant group three is made up of—
   A. Seeds
   B. Ferns
   C. Wood

5. In plant group four are—
   A. Snow and ice
   B. Hot springs
   C. Trees and grass

Writer's Corner

Look around you. Write down all the plant forms that you see, eat, or wear in one day.

Exercise 10

Jeans

"How are you fixed for school things?" Brad's dad asked him.

Brad looked up from the TV show he was watching. "School things? What kind of things?"

"Oh, pants and shirts. That sort of thing. The shirt you are wearing right now has a big hole in the sleeve," Mr. Mills said.

Brad looked at the hole, "I've been wearing this ever since school let out. When do you want to shop, Dad?"

"How about right now?" asked his dad.

"Cool," said Brad. "This isn't a very good TV show. Let's go."

The drive to the mall didn't take long. They parked the car and walked to the store. On a shelf was a pile of jeans.

"What size do you wear, Brad?" asked his dad.

"I wear a size 10," Brad told his dad.

"We'll take three pairs of jeans size 10, "Mr. Mills said to the clerk. "And four of those t-shirts and six pairs of socks. Will that do it, Brad?"

They drove home.

"I think I'll put on a pair of my new jeans," Brad said.

He tugged, and he tugged, and he tugged. He could not get them zipped. "Uh-oh," he said. "I was a size 10 last year. Now I guess I'm a size 12."

He and his dad drove back to the mall.

---

1. Brad went to the mall with his—
    A. Mom
    B. Dad
    C. Aunt

2. Brad thought his jean size was—
    A. 10
    B. 12
    C. 14

3. Brad got new jeans, t-shirts, and—
    A. Shoes
    B. Belt
    C. Socks

4. Brad's new jeans were—
    A. Too tight
    B. Too long
    C. Too loose

5. What would be the best new title?
    A. Old Jeans
    B. New Jeans
    C. Start of School

Writer's Corner

Where did your last pair of jeans go? Write about a pair of pants or a shirt that you like a lot.

Coal

Coal is a soft, black or brown rock dug from the ground. It is not used to heat homes as it once was. But it still has lots of uses. It is used to make dyes, drugs, paints, soaps, light oils, too many things to list.

We cannot count how many years it took for coal to form. Long ago the earth was young. The air was damp and hot. Most of the plants were ferns and trees. Plants died, and more plants grew on top of them. This went on year after year after year. The dead plants rotted. They turned into something that looked like soft wood. It is called peat.

After a while, large parts of the earth sank. Seas poured in. They were full of mud and sand. This mud and sand landed on top of the peat. They pressed it down, down, down. This is what turned it into coal. It took about five to eight feet of rotted plants to make one foot of coal.

Getting coal from the ground is hard work. At one time miners worked 60 hours a week. Then it was cut back to 52, then 48. Now miners work 35 hours a week.

In the days of World War II, miners worked long hours. Tons and tons of coal were needed all over the world. The miners and the coal they mined helped our land win that war.

---

1. We get coal from the—
   A. Sea
   B. Ground
   C. Air

2. Dead plants first turned into—
   A. Peat
   B. Paint
   C. Oil

3. At one time coal was—
   A. Mud and sand
   B. Ferns and trees
   C. Soaps and dyes

4. Each miner now works—
   A. 35 hours
   B. 60 hours
   C. 52 hours

5. In the days of World War II. miners—
   A. Went on strike
   B. Stayed home
   C. Worked long hours

Writer's Corner

How long do you think is fair to work per week? Write a note to your boss that tells your point of view.

Exercise 12

Nell Green

Nell woke up one day. She did not feel well. She called to her mom. Mrs. Green came right away. She was still in her robe.

"I don't want to go to school today," Nell said to her mom.

"That is not like you, Nell. You love school," said Mrs. Green.

"Well, I don't want to go today. I feel very strange," said Nell.

"Do you hurt any place?" asked her mom.

Nell thought about this. "My neck feels funny. My throat hurts."

Mrs. Green put her hand on Nell's forehead. "You feel a bit warm. You should stay in bed today. Do you want a bite to eat?"

"No," Nell said. "But I would like a cold drink."

"I will go and get dressed," said Nell's mom. "Then I will fix you something cool to drink."

Nell lay in bed while her mom was gone. She did not like to miss school. She had planned to work on her leaf scrapbook today.

Soon her mom came back into the bedroom. She handed Nell a glass of juice. It had ice chips in it.

Nell took a sip. "Ouch," she said. "That hurts."

Mrs. Green took a close look at Nell. Then she got a looking glass. She handed it to Nell. "Look at yourself," she said.

Nell looked at herself. "Oh, dear," she said. "I think I've got the mumps!"

---

1. When Nell woke up, she —
    A. Jumped out of bed
    B. Did not feel well
    C. Took a bath

2. Nell asked her mom for—
    A. A cold drink
    B. Ham and eggs
    C. A milkshake

3. Nell had planned to work on her—
    A. Star scrapbook
    B. Rock scrapbook
    C. Leaf scrapbook

4. Nell's mom brought her—
    A. Popcorn
    B. Fruit juice
    C. Hot tea

5. What was wrong with Nell?
    A. She had the flu.
    B. She had a cold.
    C. She had the mumps.

Writer's Corner

Write about a day you stayed home sick. What did you do all day?

Black Bears

Most black bears look bigger than they are. This is because they have long, coarse hair and loose skin. Bears have short, strong legs. Their toenails are long and thick. They use their nails to claw and dig. Their nails help them climb trees.

Bears eat many kinds of food. They eat small wildlife, fish, grubs, and birds' eggs. They steal lambs and young pigs from farms. Bears also seem to like fruit and nuts.

Their eyes are small so they do not see well. But they have a keen sense of smell and sound.

Black bears run very fast when they need to. If a black bear is chasing you, you should not climb a tree. Bears can zip up a tree in a flash even though they weigh a lot.

Most black bears are shy. They do not charge unless they are hurt or taking care of their young.

When it grows cold, black bears sleep a lot. They like to sleep in trees or caves. They may not stir out of their dens for months at a time. Their tiny cubs are born in the dens. The little bears stay inside the den for two months.

There are many other kinds of bears to learn about. Look for a book that tells all about bears.

---

1. Black bears look—
    A. Bigger than they are
    B. Older than they are
    C. Smaller than they are

2. Black bears cannot—
    A. See well
    B. Hear well
    C. Smell well

3. Black bears are —
    A. Bold
    B. Shy
    C. Slow

4. Baby bears stay in the den for—
    A. Two months
    B. Four months
    C. Six months

5. Black bears sleep—
    A. In back yards
    B. In trees or caves
    C. Under a bush

Writer's Corner

Bear cubs look like they would be fun to watch and hold. Write about a stuffed bear you have played with.

Exercise 14

Bats

Bats do not harm us. But some of us do not like bats. Why is this so? Is it because they come out only at night? Is it because they look like a small rat with wings? If we knew more about bats, we might not fear them so.

Bats live all over the world. They like warm lands best. They like to live in caves or under a bridge. Lots of bats live in just one place. When they find a spot they like, they stay there for years and years. Most bats eat bugs, bugs, and more bugs.

Once they have filled up on bugs, bats head for home. It is time to sleep. They hang upside down from the roof of their cave or house. Their wings are wrapped around them.

When bats try to walk on the ground, they look very funny. Their wings get in their way. Their knees bend backward, but in the air few birds can fly as well as bats.

Bats in our part of the world are only two inches long. They can spread their wings about a foot. In some places, a bat may be as long as 12 inches. Its wing span may be seven feet. Some bats fly south when it gets cold. Others just find a hole in a tree and take a long, long nap.

---

1. Bats like to live in—
   A. Warm lands
   B. The North Pole
   C. Next to a road

2. Bats like to eat—
   A. Other bats
   B. Fruit
   C. Bugs

3. When bats sleep, they—
   A. Do not close their eyes
   B. Hang upside down
   C. Stand on one foot

4. Bats have knees that—
   A. Bend forward
   B. Do not bend
   C. Bend backward

5. A bat can be as long as—
   A. 12 inches
   B. 12 feet
   C. 7 feet

Writer's Corner

Write a note to a young friend that tells why he or she should not fear bats.

Gold

We have always searched for gold. It is hard to find because gold is very rare. It can be found in the earth or in streams. It can even be found in the sea. But not in big chunks. Just a little here and a little there.

Sometimes a lot of gold is found in one place. That is called a gold field. Gold is sometimes mined like coal. It is sometimes sifted from sand and stones found in streams. It is sometimes scooped. Next it must go to a mill. There other ores are taken out. The gold is now pure.

Gold is soft. It can be formed into any shape. It can be drawn into fine wire. It does not rust. We have all heard of 24K gold. That means it is pure gold. 18K gold is a mix of gold and some other ore.

It is not known when gold was first found. Bowls made of gold that date back 5,000 years have been dug up in far lands. Many have tried to make gold. All have failed.

There was a great gold rush in 1849. Many dashed to the West Coast as fast as they could get there. Some found gold and grew rich. Many more found no gold at all and went back home.

---

1. A lot of gold in one place is called—
   A. A gold rush
   B. A gold field
   C. A gold mine

2. Gold is pure when—
   A. It first comes from the ground
   B. Other ores are taken out
   C. It is washed in a stream

3. When gold is pure, it is called—
   A. 24K gold
   B. 18K gold
   C. 16K gold

4. We know that gold was used at least—
   A. 100 years ago
   B. 5,000 years ago
   C. 500 years ago

5. The gold rush took place in—
   A. 1929
   B. 1889
   C. 1849

Writer's Corner

Would you like to pan for gold? Write what tools you would need to do so.

Exercise 16

The Beach

Jan was eating toast and jam. Her dad and mom were eating ham and eggs.

"This would be a good day to go to the beach," Jan said.

Mom and Dad smiled. "You are right, Jan." said Mom. "This is a great day to go to the beach."

Jan stood up. "I'll go get my swim suit. Can we take some food?"

"I'll pack a lunch," Mom said. "We all like to eat at the beach."

"Be sure to take bread and cheese and chips and cake," Dad said.

"And drinks, too," called Jan.

At the beach, Jan's mom spread out a rug. She sat down with a book. "You two have fun," she said. "I am going to read my book."

Jan and her dad played ball on the beach. They made a sand fort. They went in for a long swim.

"I'm starved," Jan said when they came out. "Let's have some lunch."

Her mom put the food on a cloth.

"Food tastes so good at the beach," Jan said.

"Yes, it does," said Mom. "And no dishes to wash."

"That's the best part," Jan said.

---

1. Jan and her mom and dad went to the beach—
   A. Before lunch
   B. Before breakfast
   C. After school

2. Jan's mom said she would—
   A. Change her dress
   B. Bake a cake
   C. Pack a lunch

3. At the beach Jan's mom—
   A. Read a book
   B. Took a nap
   C. Knit some socks

4. At the beach Jan and her dad—
   A. Took a walk
   B. Flew a kite
   C. Made a sand fort

5. What would be the best new title?
   A. Jan Goes for a Swim
   B. A Day at the Beach
   C. No Dishes

Writer's Corner

If you could spend the day in any place in the world, where would you go? Write why you picked that spot.

Salt

We must eat some salt each day for good health. But it also makes our food taste good. Salt has been used for a long, long time. Even cave men used salt.

Salt is found in mines under the ground. It is mined in much the same way as coal. Deep shafts are sunk in the ground. Miners go down into these shafts. They blow up walls of salt. Chunks of salt drop from the blast. These are put into small railroad cars and taken to the top.

We have learned how to take salt from the sea and from salt lakes. This is very pure salt. But getting salt this way costs a lot.

In some places, salt is found on top of the ground. Then it is called a salt lick. That is a good name. Farm stock find the pile of salt and lick it.

We use tons and tons of salt each year. It is used in canning foods or packing meats. It is also used to make things like glass and soap.

We spread salt on our roads to melt snow and ice. Farmers mix it with hay so the hay does not spoil. Best of all, it is used to help freeze ice cream!

---

1. Everyone needs salt for—
   A. Smooth skin
   B. Good health
   C. Strong bones

2. Most of our salt comes from—
   A. Mines
   B. Clouds
   C. Plants

3. Some of our salt comes from—
   A. Caves
   B. Swamps
   C. Seas and salt lakes

4. Salt found on top of the ground—
   A. Is called a salt lick
   B. Scares livestock away
   C. Spoils farm crops

5. We spread salt on roads to—
   A. Melt ice and snow
   B. Fill in bumps
   C. Make cars go faster

Writer's Corner

Salt Lake is found in the state of Utah. Use a map and write what states or towns you must pass through to get there.

Exercise 18

Seals

At one time, there were few seals left in the world. Hunters had killed them for food. They had used oil from the seals for heat and light. Then a group of world leaders had a meeting. They all said they would not kill seals any more. Now each year there are more and more seals.

There are two kinds of seals: true seals and eared seals. The true seals have no ears. They only have holes in the side of the head. True seals spend most of their life in the sea. Their young are born there. The little seal pups are white when they are born. They turn dark when they start to search for their own food. True seals do not make much noise. Just a soft growl now and then.

The eared seals do have ears. They spend more time on land than in the sea. Their pups are born on land. Eared seals roar and bark and howl and bleat. It is not hard to tell when a crowd of loud eared seals is nearby.

True seals and eared seals are about the same shape. Some are gray. Some are brown. Some may have dark spots or bands. Some say that eared seals are smarter than true seals. They can be taught to play games and do tricks.

---

1. The two kinds of seals are—
   A. Big and small seals
   B. True and eared seals
   C. Black and white seals

2. Seals were saved when—
   A. They moved to the South Pole
   B. They hid under the ice
   C. World leaders made new rules

3. At birth seal pups are—
   A. White
   B. Black
   C. Striped

4. True seals do not—
   A. Make much noise
   B. Live in the sea
   C. Have grey/brown fur

5. Eared seals can be taught to—
   A. Run away
   B. Play games and do tricks
   C. Chase true seals

Writer's Corner

Seals were saved thanks to folks who cared. Write to a state wildlife group to help save a species you care about.

Skunks

Have you ever been near a skunk? It is not a good place to be!

In our land, we call a skunk a skunk. In some lands, it is called a polecat. A skunk is small. It is about the size of large cat. It has a long nose that ends in a point. Its legs are short. The skunk has a funny walk. It walks as if its feet hurt.

The fur of a skunk is long and thick and black. It has a white stripe down its back. A skunk also has a small white patch on its forehead and on its tail.

A skunk's very bad smell comes from a pair of glands near its tail. In the glands is stored something wet and sticky. When the skunk gets scared, look out! In a flash, he squirts out the smelly stuff. Everyone runs and keeps on running. The smell is hard to get rid of. It seems to cling to hair and clothes for a long time.

Skunks look for trees that have holes in them. That is where they make their homes. They eat bugs and mice. They love to eat raw eggs. They sneak into barns and steal them.

Their thick fur was once used for coats. Now fur coats are not worn as much as they used to be. So skunks are safe.

---

1. A skunk has—
   A. Four white feet
   B. A white stripe down its back
   C. A white nose

2. When a skunk is scared, it—
   A. Hides
   B. Runs away
   C. Squirts smelly stuff

3. Skunks make their homes in—
   A. Trees
   B. Caves
   C. Ditches

4. Another name for skunk is—
   A. Kitty
   B. Polecat
   C. Wildcat

5. A skunk's fur was once used for—
   A. Rugs
   B. Pants
   C. Coats

Writer's Corner

Skunks can fight back when they get scared. Write about what you would do to keep yourself from harm.

Exercise 20

Splash!

Max and Sue went out to play. It was a nice day with lots of sun. But it had rained the day before.

"Look at that wet mud in the street," Max said.

"Don't jump in it, Max," said Sue.

Max had a gleam in his eye. "I will not jump in it. I will throw a rock in it."

Sue said, "No! That is a bad plan."

"Just one little old rock," said Max. He looked at the ground. He saw a rock. He picked it up. He hid it behind his back.

Then he said, "Oh, Sue, look at that fat white cloud."

Sue looked up at the sky. Splash went the rock. Small bits of mud flew this way and that.

Max began to laugh. "Ha! Look at yourself, Sue! There is a chunk of mud on your cheek."

Sue got mad. "Cut it out, Max! Just look at my new coat. It's got mud all over it. I am going inside."

She ran up the steps and into the house.

"Girls! They are no fun at all!" Max said. He picked up two more rocks. He tossed one into the wet mud. Splash! Then he did it again. Splash! Why was it not fun anymore?

Max ran into the house. "Sue," he called. "Do you want to play some ball?"

---

1. Max and Sue went out to—
    A. Weed
    B. Skate
    C. Play

2. Max and Sue saw a—
    A. Mud puddle
    B. Rainbow
    C. Snow drift

3. Mud splashed on Sue's—
    A. Socks
    B. Coat
    C. Shoes

4. Sue ran into the—
    A. House
    B. Street
    C. Barn

5. You can tell that Max—
    A. Did not like to play alone
    B. Did not want to play with Sue again
    C. Was glad Sue had gone inside

Writer's Corner

What Max did to Sue was mean. Write a note to Max or to Sue that tells how you feel.

Sharks

Sharks can be found in all the seas of the world. They like the warm seas best. Now and then, sharks have been found in lakes. But not the whale shark. It is 50 feet long. It needs lots of room so it stays in the deep seas.

Not all sharks are the same. There are 250 kinds of sharks. But they are all the same in one way. They like to eat and eat and eat. They spend most of their time looking for food. Most any kind of food. A shark does not care if it is a fish or a plant. Just so it is food. Even seals have to stay clear of sharks.

Sharks swim fast. They can swim after ships for days and days. They will not give up. They wait for food to be tossed over the back of the ship. They seem to know that leftovers will be flung into the sea. Then their wide mouths scoop up the food. That wide mouth is on the underside of the shark's head. A shark may lose a tooth from time to time. Then a new tooth grows in its place.

Sharks have been known to swim near a beach. Then signs are put up. The signs say, "TAKE CARE. A SHARK HAS BEEN SEEN NEAR THIS BEACH!"

---

1. Sharks can be found—
   A. Only in lakes
   B. Only in streams
   C. In all the world's seas

2. A shark spends most of its time—
   A. Chasing whales
   B. Looking for food
   C. Scaring swimmers

3. Now and then sharks have been found in a—
   A. Pond
   B. Swimming pool
   C. Lake

4. A shark's mouth is on—
   A. The underside of its head
   B. The top of its head
   C. The ends of its ears

5. Signs on a beach—
   A. Make sharks stay away
   B. Warn swimmers
   C. Say no surf boards

Writer's Corner

"Jaws" is a film that made people fear sharks. Write about a film that scared you.

Exercise 22

Oil

It would be hard to live without oil. We use oil in lots of ways. We need it to run our cars and trucks and planes. That kind of oil comes from deep in the ground. It can also be found under the sea.

Some of the oil we use in our cars and planes comes from lands far away. It is shipped in big boats. Inside the boats are large tanks. These tanks hold the oil. Now and then, one of the large boats will hit a sand bar. This could make its tanks split and leak. The oil could float to a shore. It kills fish and wild life. Helpers come from near and far to help clean up the mess. It can take years to get the shore clean again.

We use oil to cook our food. This is not the same kind of oil we use in our cars. This oil comes from plants. We get oil from corn. We even get oil from trees. One of these trees grows in a land over the sea. It is shaped like a boot. Do you know what land that is?

The palm tree also gives oil. Palm oil makes fine soap. It can be mixed with grain and then fed to cows. It can be used to make paint.

Can you think of the ways you use oil at your house?

---

1. We could not run our cars without—
   A. Oil
   B. Ice cream
   C. Popcorn

2. Inside an oil tanker are—
   A. Large tanks of oil
   B. Bowls of oil
   C. Jugs of oil

3. Which is true?
   A. It takes years to clean up an oil spill.
   B. Oil spills are good for fish.
   C. Oil spills do not harm beaches.

4. We get some oil from—
   A. Wheat
   B. Corn
   C. Rice

5. A tree that gives oil is the—
   A. Palm tree
   B. Oak tree
   C. Peach tree

Writer's Corner

Labs are testing new fuels to run cars, such as wind or sun or plants. Write about what you would use to make fuel.

Exercise 23

Grapes

Grapes are a fruit with smooth skin that grows on a vine. They are grown in mild parts of the world. We eat them fresh, dried, and in juice. In many places they are grown for wine.

Old World grapes were brought to the New World. No one knows quite when. The days were too hot for them in the South. The days were too cold for them in the North. At last, it was found that they would grow well on the West Coast.

There are now about 3,000 kinds of grapes. They are grown and picked in bunches. They are sometimes deep red, sometimes black. Most often grapes are green.

Grapevines are shrubs that climb. The main stem is the *trunk*. Each vine trunk must be held up by a strong stake. The main branch is called an *arm*. The soft new growths are called *shoots*. Grape leaves are thin and quite large. They are smooth on one side with fuzz on the other side. Grapes can have one to four seeds. Some have no seeds at all.

There are bugs that hurt the grape vines. There is also black rot that strikes the fruit itself. Grape growers must spray and dust to keep these pests away from their crops. To get the best grapes, they must also prune the vines each year.

---

1. Grapes grow—
   A. On a tree
   B. On a vine
   C. In the ground

2. In this country grapes grow well in the—
   A. South
   B. North
   C. West

3. The stem of the grape vine is called the—
   A. Shoots
   B. Arm
   C. Trunk

4. The main branch of the grape vine is called the—
   A. Shoots
   B. Arm
   C. Trunk

5. The soft new growth of the grape vine is called the—
   A. Shoots
   B. Arm
   C. Trunk

Writer's Corner

Write an ad for grape juice that will make someone want to buy it.

Exercise 24

The Ditch

One day Mr. Jones woke up. He looked outside. "What a fine day. I think I will go for a walk."

He put on his clothes. Then he ate a meal. He grabbed his cane and started off. He walked in the woods near his house for an hour. Then he walked in the park. He was on his way back to his house when a man on a bike shot by. Mr. Jones jumped out of the way. He fell into a deep ditch. The man on the bike did not stop.

"Ouch!" Mr. Jones said out loud. He tried to stand up. He could not. His left leg hurt. He lay there for a long time. How was he going to get out of that ditch? Now and then he called out,

"Help! Help!"

At last two boys came by the ditch. They heard the yells. They looked down and saw Mr. Jones. One of the boys jumped into the ditch.

"I will help you stand up," the boy said. "Then my pal will pull you out of the ditch."

The plan worked well. Soon Mr. Jones was out of the ditch. "Thank you, boys," he said. "I want to give you some cash."

"No, thank you," said one of the boys. "Some day I could fall into a ditch. Then I would want someone to help me."

---

1. Mr. Jones thought he would—
    A. Take a nap
    B. Wash his clothes
    C. Go for a walk

2. First Mr. Jones walked—
    A. In the woods
    B. On a busy street
    C. Near a lake

3. Mr. Jones fell into a—
    A. Patch of mud
    B. Pond
    C. Ditch

4. Mr. Jones was helped by—
    A. Two boys
    B. Two girls
    C. A man on a bike

5. Mr. Jones wanted to give the boys—
    A. A ride home
    B. Some cash
    C. A free meal

Writer's Corner

Did you ever have have a chance to help someone in need? Write about that time.

Frogs and Toads

Frogs and toads are not the same. The skin of a toad has bumps. The skin of a frog does not. We find toads on land. Frogs like ponds and lakes.

Frogs and toads are the same in one way. They both start as tadpoles. The frog or toad lays some eggs. The egg turns into a tadpole. It is very small. In ten days it grows a tail. In four weeks it has legs. At first, it uses its gills to take in air. Then the gills go away. The tadpole grows lungs. It starts to turn green. Its tail goes away. It is about eight weeks old. Now it looks like a very small frog or toad.

Frogs and toads have to eat a lot before snow falls. They try to get fat.

Then they look for a spot to sleep. A hole in deep mud in a pond makes a fine home. The top of the pond may turn into ice. But frogs and toads know that their bed of mud will stay damp and soft.

As they sleep, their hearts beat slow. Their lungs shut down. Their skin now takes in the air they need.

One day spring comes. It is time for the frogs and toads to wake up. How do they know this?

---

1. How are frogs and toads not the same?
   A. Toads have bumps; frogs do not.
   B. Toads are green; frogs are black.
   C. Toads have lungs; frogs do not.

2. How are frogs and toads the same?
   A. They both like ponds and lakes.
   B. They both start as tadpoles.
   C. They both have smooth skin.

3. Before snow falls, frogs and toads—
   A. Look for a spot to sleep
   B. Stop eating
   C. Grow new skin

4. A bed of mud is a good place because—
   A. It dries up.
   B. It has lots of noise.
   C. It stays damp and soft.

5. In the spring, frogs and toads—
   A. Go to sleep
   B. Wake up
   C. Shed their skin

Writer's Corner

What if you were a frog or toad in a mud hole? Write what you would do on the spring day when you wake up.

Exercise 26

The Mole

A mole spends most of his life underground. This is where he finds his food. He loves grubs and worms. Underground is the best spot to find these treats. Every 24 hours the poor mole must eat his own weight in food. If he can't find food for 12 hours, he will die. So his search must go on day and night. This may be why he seems so mean and tense.

The mole may be small but he likes a good fight. Small wildlife try to stay out of his way. His fur is soft. His pink tail is about an inch long. He has no neck. His ears are too small to be seen. In the past, moles were thought to be blind. They are not. They can see, but not very well. Their small eyes are hard to find through flaps of fur and skin.

A mole has large front paws and sharp strong teeth. These are his best tools. With them he can dig an underground path. He can dig a path as long as 225 feet in one night.

The mole is a great help to us when he eats bugs that feed on crops. He is not a great help when his underground paths make big bumps in our prized green lawns.

---

1. The mole spends most of his life—
   A. Under water
   B. In the snow
   C. Underground

2. A mole must have food at least—
   A. Every 24 hours
   B. Every 12 hours
   C. Every 2 days

3. The mole is small but he—
   A. Likes a good fight
   B. Is shy and meek
   C. Only fights at night

4. A mole has large front paws but small—
   A. Eyes
   B. Teeth
   C. Nose

5. In one night a mole can dig a path—
   A. 22 feet long
   B. 225 feet long
   C. 25 feet long

Writer's Corner

"Mole" also means spy. Write the plot for a TV show with a spy in the lead role.

Ants

If you see one ant, you will soon see lots of ants. All ants live in groups. Each group has three sorts of ants – the males, the queen, and the workers. Everything is planned. Every ant has a job to do.

The queen ant lays eggs. That's all she does. She can live as long as 15 years.

The worker ants live just to serve the queen and the rest of the ants in the group. They bring in the food. They build rooms in the nest. They keep these rooms very clean. If a speck of trash drops, a worker will rush to take it out. Ants can't stand dirt!

Workers can have more than one job. There is a kind of worker who has a huge head and strong jaws. His job is to grind up grain in his mouth. But when he has ground all the grain, his head is bitten off! He is of no more use to the group.

Some ants do not have a nest. They march in one line from place to place. If a house is in their path, they eat their way through it.

There are ants who keep herds of plant lice. They stroke the sides of these lice until a kind of milk comes out. The ants love this milk. They take very good care of the lice. They keep them warm when it is cold outside. They take them into the sunshine when spring comes.

---

1. The queen ant can live as long as—
    A. 15 years
    B. 18 years
    C. 25 years

2. The queen ant's job is to—
    A. Bring in food
    B. Clean the nest
    C. Lay eggs

3. After the worker has ground up all the grain—
    A. His head is bitten off
    B. He is given a chance to rest
    C. He is sent out to search for more grain

4. You can tell that—
    A. Ants like to work
    B. Ants do not like to work
    C. Ants like to live alone

5. Ants love milk that comes from—
    A. Cows
    B. Lice
    C. Goats

Writer's Corner

If ants were in charge, the world would be very neat. What are some things you think we can learn from ants?

Exercise 28

The Card

Ted was not poor. He was not rich. He got pay from his job each week. He used his pay for his rent and food. There was not much left.

Ted wanted to go out and have fun. But he had little cash. So he stayed at home. He turned on his old TV. He watched it for a few hours. Then he went to bed.

This boring life went on for a long time. Then one day a bank sent him a card. He could use the card to buy things. But he would not have to pay for them.

What fun! Ted got a new suit. He saw a TV in a store. He went in and bought it. He took a trip on a plane. One day he fell in love with a boat. "Why not?" he asked himself. The boat store was closed. He would come back the next day. He went home.

In his mailbox was a bill. It had a list of all the things he had bought. It told how much he would have to pay for these things.

"Uh-oh," said Ted. "It will take a long time to pay off this bill."

He took out his card. He cut it in two. "From now on I will buy with cash," said Ted. And he did.

---

1. Ted used his pay from his job for—
   A. A big car
   B. His rent and food
   C. Trips

2. A bank sent Ted—
   A. A letter
   B. A card
   C. Some blank checks

3. Ted used the card to pay for—
   A. His rent
   B. A TV set
   C. His food

4. The boat store—
   A. Was open
   B. Had burned down
   C. Was closed

5. Ted took out his card and—
   A. Cut it in two
   B. Mailed it back to the bank
   C. Gave it to a friend

Writer's Corner

Write a savings plan for cash that you earn or get. Set a goal to save a bit each month.

Exercise 29

Moss

Moss looks like a soft green pad. It seems to be just one plant. A close look shows that it is made up of lots and lots of little plants. There are about 14,000 kinds of mosses all over the world.

Mosses do not grow very tall. And they look as if they are not very strong. Not so! They can grow in all sorts of odd places. One kind of moss grows 100 feet deep in a lake. Another kind lives far north. It lies under the snow most of the year. Mosses can be found in most swamps. The only place moss cannot live is in a sea that has salt in it.

A moss plant does not have roots. It does not have stems or leaves. Some mosses have small yellow spots. These are spores. When ripe, the spores break away from the plant. They float through the air on a breeze. When they land in the right spot, a new rug of moss will sprout. All they need is a bit of very damp soil.

Have you heard of peat? It is dug up in chunks in swamps and bogs. It is then burned for heat in cold places where there is little wood. Peat is formed from stacks and stacks of moss. It takes years and years to make peat moss.

---

1. How many different kinds of mosses are there?
   A. 140
   B. 14,000
   C. 1,400

2. The only place moss cannot live is—
   A. In a salty sea
   B. Under snow
   C. In swamps

3. Some mosses have small yellow spots called—
   A. Roots
   B. Stems
   C. Spores

4. The moss spores need—
   A. Dry soil
   B. Damp soil
   C. Stormy weather

5. You can tell that peat moss—
   A. Burns well
   B. Can be eaten for lunch
   C. Can be fed to livestock

Writer's Corner

No one plants moss, it just grows on its own. Write about other plants that grow this way.

Exercise 30

Snakes

Snakes can be found in all parts of the world. Some live on land and in the earth. Some live in the sea or in trees.

There are about 3,000 kinds of snakes. Most of them are harmless. But some can kill. They strike out and bite with their fangs. A rattlesnake is this kind of killer. It gets its name from a noise at the end of its tail. Rattlesnakes can be found in just about all of our states.

Most snakes lay eggs. The snake finds a hole in a pile of leaves or in a tree. There she lays her eggs. Now and then she leaves them. She finds some bright sunlight. When she is warm, she goes back to her eggs. In this way she keeps them warm.

The snake leaves when the eggs start to hatch. Their shells are soft and white. Each small snake has a spike on its nose. It uses this spike to rip and tear the shell. It takes an hour to get out of the shell. Then the small snake is on its own. It must feed itself from the first day. The spike falls off in two or three days.

Snakes feed on rats, mice, moles, frogs, and bugs. That makes them our good friends.

---

1. How many kinds of snakes are there?
   A. 3,000
   B. 300
   C. 30

2. Rattlesnakes can be found—
   A. In just a few states
   B. Only in one state
   C. In almost every state

3. A snake lays eggs—
   A. In the street
   B. In a hole
   C. In a pail

4. A baby snake can get out of its shell in—
   A. An hour
   B. A day
   C. A week

5. Why are snakes our good friends?
   A. They eat weeds.
   B. They eat rats, mice, and bugs.
   C. They eat other snakes.

Writer's Corner

Have you seen a snake up close in the wild or in a tank? Write about how you felt when you saw it.

ANSWER KEY

Title	Page	Title	Page	Title	Page
Rain	1	**Goats**	7	**Black Bears**	13
1. A		1. A		1. A	
2. B		2. C		2. A	
3. A		3. C		3. B	
4. A		4. B		4. A	
5. B		5. A		5. B	
The Sale	2	**The Trunk**	8	**Bats**	14
1. B		1. B		1. A	
2. B		2. B		2. C	
3. A		3. A		3. B	
4. B		4. C		4. C	
5. C		5. B		5. A	
Roads	3	**Plants**	9	**Gold**	15
1. B		1. A		1. B	
2. C		2. C		2. B	
3. A		3. A		3. A	
4. A		4. B		4. B	
5. A		5. C		5. C	
The Doghouse	4	**Jeans**	10	**The Beach**	16
1. B		1. B		1. A	
2. A		2. A		2. C	
3. B		3. C		3. A	
4. A		4. A		4. C	
5. A		5. B		5. B	
Rice	5	**Coal**	11	**Salt**	17
1. B		1. B		1. B	
2. C		2. A		2. A	
3. A		3. B		3. C	
4. B		4. A		4. A	
5. C		5. C		5. A	
The Fireplace	6	**Nell Green**	12	**Seals**	18
1. B		1. B		1. B	
2. A		2. A		2. C	
3. B		3. C		3. A	
4. B		4. B		4. A	
5. C		5. C		5. B	

High Noon Reading Fluency, Level A

ANSWER KEY (continued)

Title	Page	Title	Page
Skunks 1. B 2. C 3. A 4. B 5. C	19	Frogs & Toads 1. A 2. B 3. A 4. C 5. B	25
Splash! 1. C 2. A 3. B 4. A 5. A	20	The Mole 1. C 2. B 3. A 4. A 5. B	26
Sharks 1. C 2. B 3. C 4. A 5. B	21	Ants 1. A 2. C 3. A 4. A 5. B	27
Oil 1. A 2. A 3. A 4. B 5. A	22	The Card 1. B 2. B 3. B 4. C 5. A	28
Grapes 1. B 2. C 3. C 4. B 5. A	23	Moss 1. B 2. A 3. C 4. B 5. A	29
The Ditch 1. C 2. A 3. C 4. A 5. B	24	Snakes 1. A 2. C 3. B 4. A 5. B	30

Answer Sheet

Name _____

Exercise # _____
Min/sec: _____
1. Ⓐ Ⓑ Ⓒ
2. Ⓐ Ⓑ Ⓒ
3. Ⓐ Ⓑ Ⓒ
4. Ⓐ Ⓑ Ⓒ
5. Ⓐ Ⓑ Ⓒ
Correct _____

Exercise # _____
Min/sec: _____
1. Ⓐ Ⓑ Ⓒ
2. Ⓐ Ⓑ Ⓒ
3. Ⓐ Ⓑ Ⓒ
4. Ⓐ Ⓑ Ⓒ
5. Ⓐ Ⓑ Ⓒ
Correct _____

Exercise # _____
Min/sec: _____
1. Ⓐ Ⓑ Ⓒ
2. Ⓐ Ⓑ Ⓒ
3. Ⓐ Ⓑ Ⓒ
4. Ⓐ Ⓑ Ⓒ
5. Ⓐ Ⓑ Ⓒ
Correct _____

Exercise # _____
Min/sec: _____
1. Ⓐ Ⓑ Ⓒ
2. Ⓐ Ⓑ Ⓒ
3. Ⓐ Ⓑ Ⓒ
4. Ⓐ Ⓑ Ⓒ
5. Ⓐ Ⓑ Ⓒ
Correct _____

Exercise # _____
Min/sec: _____
1. Ⓐ Ⓑ Ⓒ
2. Ⓐ Ⓑ Ⓒ
3. Ⓐ Ⓑ Ⓒ
4. Ⓐ Ⓑ Ⓒ
5. Ⓐ Ⓑ Ⓒ
Correct _____

Exercise # _____
Min/sec: _____
1. Ⓐ Ⓑ Ⓒ
2. Ⓐ Ⓑ Ⓒ
3. Ⓐ Ⓑ Ⓒ
4. Ⓐ Ⓑ Ⓒ
5. Ⓐ Ⓑ Ⓒ
Correct _____

Exercise # _____
Min/sec: _____
1. Ⓐ Ⓑ Ⓒ
2. Ⓐ Ⓑ Ⓒ
3. Ⓐ Ⓑ Ⓒ
4. Ⓐ Ⓑ Ⓒ
5. Ⓐ Ⓑ Ⓒ
Correct _____

Exercise # _____
Min/sec: _____
1. Ⓐ Ⓑ Ⓒ
2. Ⓐ Ⓑ Ⓒ
3. Ⓐ Ⓑ Ⓒ
4. Ⓐ Ⓑ Ⓒ
5. Ⓐ Ⓑ Ⓒ
Correct _____

Exercise # _____
Min/sec: _____
1. Ⓐ Ⓑ Ⓒ
2. Ⓐ Ⓑ Ⓒ
3. Ⓐ Ⓑ Ⓒ
4. Ⓐ Ⓑ Ⓒ
5. Ⓐ Ⓑ Ⓒ
Correct _____

Exercise # _____
Min/sec: _____
1. Ⓐ Ⓑ Ⓒ
2. Ⓐ Ⓑ Ⓒ
3. Ⓐ Ⓑ Ⓒ
4. Ⓐ Ⓑ Ⓒ
5. Ⓐ Ⓑ Ⓒ
Correct _____

Exercise # _____
Min/sec: _____
1. Ⓐ Ⓑ Ⓒ
2. Ⓐ Ⓑ Ⓒ
3. Ⓐ Ⓑ Ⓒ
4. Ⓐ Ⓑ Ⓒ
5. Ⓐ Ⓑ Ⓒ
Correct _____

Exercise # _____
Min/sec: _____
1. Ⓐ Ⓑ Ⓒ
2. Ⓐ Ⓑ Ⓒ
3. Ⓐ Ⓑ Ⓒ
4. Ⓐ Ⓑ Ⓒ
5. Ⓐ Ⓑ Ⓒ
Correct _____

WORDS PER MINUTE LOG

(Graph with y-axis values: 0, 25, 50, 75, 100, 125, 150, 175, 200, 225, 250)

Exercise ___ ___ ___ ___ ___ ___ ___ ___ ___ ___ ___ ___
WPM* ___ ___ ___ ___ ___ ___ ___ ___ ___ ___ ___ ___

*See Words Per Minute Chart on pages 42–43

Copyright © 2004 by High Noon Books. Permission granted to reproduce for classroom use. **High Noon Reading Fluency, Level A**

Words Per Minute Chart

To find Words Per Minute, find the lesson number on the side of the chart. Then find the time closest to your time at the top of the chart. The point where the row and column meet tells the number of Words Per Minute that you read. Record this number on your Answer Sheet.

Lesson Number	Number of Words	Time										
		1:00	1:05	1:10	1:15	1:20	1:25	1:30	1:35	1:40	1:45	1:50	1:55
1	201	201	186	172	161	151	142	134	127	121	115	110	105
2	228	228	210	195	182	171	161	152	144	137	130	124	119
3	235	235	217	201	188	176	166	157	148	141	134	128	123
4	212	212	196	182	170	159	150	141	134	127	121	116	111
5	217	217	200	186	174	163	153	145	137	130	124	118	113
6	224	224	207	192	179	168	158	149	141	134	128	122	117
7	248	248	229	213	198	186	175	165	157	149	142	135	129
8	229	229	211	196	183	172	162	153	145	137	131	125	119
9	216	216	199	185	173	162	152	144	136	130	123	118	113
10	222	222	205	190	178	167	157	148	140	133	127	121	116
11	239	239	221	205	191	179	169	159	151	143	137	130	125
12	231	231	213	198	185	173	163	154	146	139	132	126	121
13	218	218	201	187	174	164	154	145	138	131	125	119	114
14	229	229	211	196	183	172	162	153	145	137	131	125	119
15	219	219	202	188	175	164	155	146	138	131	125	119	114
16	200	200	185	171	160	150	141	133	126	120	114	109	104
17	210	210	194	180	168	158	148	140	133	126	120	115	110
18	223	223	206	191	178	167	157	149	141	134	127	122	116
19	229	229	211	196	183	172	162	153	145	137	131	125	119
20	224	224	207	192	179	168	158	149	141	134	128	122	117
21	223	223	206	191	178	167	157	149	141	134	127	122	116
22	234	234	216	201	187	176	165	156	148	140	134	128	122
23	225	225	208	193	180	169	159	150	142	135	129	123	117
24	230	230	212	197	184	173	162	153	145	138	131	125	120
25	219	219	202	188	175	164	155	146	138	131	125	119	114
26	218	218	201	187	174	164	154	145	138	131	125	119	114
27	247	247	228	212	198	185	174	165	156	148	141	135	129
28	224	224	207	192	179	168	158	149	141	134	128	122	117
29	226	226	209	194	181	170	160	151	143	136	129	123	118
30	216	216	199	185	173	162	152	144	136	130	123	118	113

To find Words Per Minute for times shorter than 1 minute and longer than 5 minutes, multiply the Number of Words in the passage (from column 2 of the chart) by 60. Then divide by your reading time (in seconds). For example, if you read a 212 word passage in 5 minutes, 20 seconds, you would perform this calculation:
212 words X 60 / 320 seconds = 40 Words Per Minute.

Words Per Minute Chart

To find Words Per Minute, find the lesson number on the side of the chart. Then find the time closest to your time at the top of the chart. The point where the row and column meet tells the number of Words Per Minute that you read. Record this number on your Answer Sheet.

Lesson Number	Time												
	2:00	2:10	2:20	2:30	2:40	2:50	3:00	3:20	3:40	4:00	4:20	4:40	5:00
1	101	93	86	80	75	71	67	60	55	50	46	43	40
2	114	105	98	91	86	80	76	68	62	57	53	49	46
3	118	108	101	94	88	83	78	71	64	59	54	50	47
4	106	98	91	85	80	75	71	64	58	53	49	45	42
5	109	100	93	87	81	77	72	65	59	54	50	47	43
6	112	103	96	90	84	79	75	67	61	56	52	48	45
7	124	114	106	99	93	88	83	74	68	62	57	53	50
8	115	106	98	92	86	81	76	69	62	57	53	49	46
9	108	100	93	86	81	76	72	65	59	54	50	46	43
10	111	102	95	89	83	78	74	67	61	56	51	48	44
11	120	110	102	96	90	84	80	72	65	60	55	51	48
12	116	107	99	92	87	82	77	69	63	58	53	50	46
13	109	101	93	87	82	77	73	65	59	55	50	47	44
14	115	106	98	92	86	81	76	69	62	57	53	49	46
15	110	101	94	88	82	77	73	66	60	55	51	47	44
16	100	92	86	80	75	71	67	60	55	50	46	43	40
17	105	97	90	84	79	74	70	63	57	53	48	45	42
18	112	103	96	89	84	79	74	67	61	56	51	48	45
19	115	106	98	92	86	81	76	69	62	57	53	49	46
20	112	103	96	90	84	79	75	67	61	56	52	48	45
21	112	103	96	89	84	79	74	67	61	56	51	48	45
22	117	108	100	94	88	83	78	70	64	59	54	50	47
23	113	104	96	90	84	79	75	68	61	56	52	48	45
24	115	106	99	92	86	81	77	69	63	58	53	49	46
25	110	101	94	88	82	77	73	66	60	55	51	47	44
26	109	101	93	87	82	77	73	65	59	55	50	47	44
27	124	114	106	99	93	87	82	74	67	62	57	53	49
28	112	103	96	90	84	79	75	67	61	56	52	48	45
29	113	104	97	90	85	80	75	68	62	57	52	48	45
30	108	100	93	86	81	76	72	65	59	54	50	46	43

To find Words Per Minute for times shorter than 1 minute and longer than 5 minutes, multiply the Number of Words in the passage (from column 2 of the chart) by 60. Then divide by your reading time (in seconds). For example, if you read a 212 word passage in 5 minutes, 20 seconds, you would perform this calculation:
212 words X 60 / 320 seconds = 40 Words Per Minute.